BLOOD

Michael Schmeltzer

Two Sylvias Press

Two Sylvias Press
PO Box 1524
Kingston, WA 98346
twosylviaspress@gmail.com

Cover Artist: Frederic Fontenoy (http://www.fredericfontenoy.com)
Cover Design: Kelli Russell Agodon
Book Design: Annette Spaulding-Convy
Author Photo: Lydia Maria S.

Created with the belief that *great writing is good for the world*, Two
Sylvias Press mixes modern technology, classic style, and literary intellect
with an eco-friendly heart. We draw our inspiration from the poetic
literary talent of Sylvia Plath and the editorial business sense of Sylvia
Beach. We are an independent press dedicated to publishing the
exceptional voices of writers.

For more information about Two Sylvias Press or to learn more about the
eBook version of *Blood Song* please visit: www.twosylviaspress.com

First Edition. Created in the United States of America.

ISBN-13: 978-0692577158
ISBN-10: 0692577157

Two Sylvias Press
www.twosylviaspress.com

Praise For *Blood Song*

There is a radical nostalgia at the heart of *Blood Song*, a nostalgia that recovers the wounds of experience and brings it to a rich, imaginative culmination. In this way, the book's title is profoundly apt: on the one hand, Michael Schmeltzer's poems are about blood and the tragic consciousness that is the result of our being in time; on the other hand, the poems are about song, the reconciling artfulness that is the source of the best poetry. As one of Schmeltzer's canny speakers says, *I know / better. I'm no better.* Equally unsettling and ravishing, *Blood Song* is a terrific debut.
— Rick Barot, author of *Chord*

ॐ

In Michael Schmeltzer's *Blood Song* we are confronted with the thrumming and violent fact of the body's music. From the haunting image of a father's wounded stomach, the metamorphosis of hornets into syringes, and the consolation passed to a grieving parent, we emerge from the book able to name our ghosts. Schmeltzer's poems are haunting love songs sung to children before sleep in the face of all the world's calamities. Poem after poem of this startling debut is filled with a tenderness capable of *turning us to tinder.*
— Oliver de la Paz, author of *Post Subject: A Fable*

ॐ

Blood Song is a perfect title for Michael Schmeltzer's powerful first book. Blood spills out of a man's slashed belly *like an open cocoon.* Blood ties family together, for good or ill. *If you turn tragedy into story / you can survive it* sounds like a prayer, but the tongue can't be trusted, words slip from one to another: *scream* to *squirm, insect* to *inflict, hear and know* to *here and now.* Familiar consolations fail: *How swiftly music / turns to stench; the things we cherish / how quickly they fly out of reach.* And: *Not every movement is dance, / not everything swallowed sustenance.* Images of salvation quickly become something else—a child freed from a closet's darkness sees *the bright blue throb of blue sky / with one cloud / marring it, / a dead dove / in the mouth of sky.* It is no small thing, then, when the speaker looks around himself and says, *None of us are dead yet.* This is a vision of what it is to be human that doesn't flinch from the hardest truths of what that includes: violence and rage and pain, but also tenderness and humor, innocence as well as experience. The poems themselves are evidence of the hard-won pleasures of making something of all that: making work, making love, making a family, making a meaningful life.

— Sharon Bryan, author of *Sharp Stars*

❧

In *Blood Song,* elegy continually resurrects the shadows, echoes, and misplaced memories of loss. Here, clouds cross the sky like a funeral procession, words brighten in the mouth, and children both bless and burn the innocence that most resembles them. Story is what we make of our survival, Schmeltzer tells us—we who see our sorrows hatching in each line. We who set fire to the nest as if the light we see could save us.

— Traci Brimhall, author of *Our Lady of the Ruins*

❧

Schmeltzer's poems wonder at the world as they grasp for the sacred, which may or may not be discovered. As the speaker states in "Elegy/Elk River," *I've been here most of*

my life // and am no less lost. A keen-eyed biography boring into the cruelties we endure and inflict upon each other and ourselves, *Blood Song* sings with vibrant imagery and euphonic music. A familial vein interweaves these poems which stir us to wonder, what darknesses do we inherit as we hum along in our *minor key of existence*?
— Matt Rasmussen, author of *Black Aperture*

Acknowledgements

The author wishes to thank the editors of the following periodicals in which some of the poems, occasionally in different forms, were first published or are forthcoming.

42 Opus: "Alterations"

Baltimore Review: "Because Your Father Died on Our Anniversary"

Bat City Review: "Kite"

Bellingham Review: "Blessing of Scabs"

Blue Earth Review: "Lighthouse"

Briar Cliff Review: "A Subtle Collapse"

Briar Cliff Review: "On the Branch a Bird We Bid Goodbye"

Crab Creek Review: "Inherited Music"

Crab Creek Review: "Elegy/Elk River"

Devil's Lake Journal: "Tsunami"

Gulf Stream: "Boil"

Hawai'i Pacific Review: "Spider Weaver"

Hawai'i Pacific Review: "What Never Breaks"

Inch: "Portrait of My Father, Shirtless"

Jelly Bucket: "Insect, Inflict"

Los Angeles Review: "Blizzard, 1996"

Many Mountains Moving: "Elegy/Tongue"

Natural Bridge: "Some Nights the Stars They Sour"

New Guard Literary Review: "Road Trip, 1983"

Noble Gas Quarterly: "Isaac Newton's Teeth"

pacificREVIEW: "Phoenix-Tongue"

Redactions: Poetry & Poetics: "The Memory of Glass"

Relief Journal: "Elegy/Sound"

Rougarou: "On One Hand Hillsides and Houses"

Southern Indiana Review: "Life Sentence"

Stickman Review: "Rituals of Comfort"

Stringtown: "Forest of No Treasure"

Sundog Lit: "Mesrobians Go Thrifting"

Vinyl: "Elegy/Echo"

Water~Stone Review: "Residue"

Water~Stone Review: "Deep Wound Singing"

The author would like to thank Floating Bridge Press, who published *Elegy/Elk River*, winner of the 2015 Floating

Bridge Press Chapbook Award, in which some of these poems appear.

To Lydia, the song I listen for and never tire of, thank you for every note, off-key and all.

To Isadora and Sophiana, my dearest instruments, I wish you every major chord of happiness this world has to offer.

To Meghan McClure, whom I trust to tune my every word, thank you for listening all these years.

To Stan Rubin and Judith Kitchen, not only for giving me a community I never knew I wanted but for reinforcing what is true and meaningful within the writing world, a chorus of gratitude and appreciation. And to the Rainier Writing Workshop, with a special nod to the pioneer class of 2007, here's to our songs and the many more to come.

To my mentors Sharon Bryan, Lola Haskins, and Kevin Clark, who gave me the sheet music, taught me the key signatures, and showed me how to improvise, a standing ovation to you all for as long as I write.

To Traci Brimhall, Rick Barot, Oliver de la Paz, and Matt Rasmussen, who lead me by example, thank you repeatedly and humbly for your words, wisdom, and generosity. I echo with gratitude.

Finally, to Kelli and Annette of Two Sylvias Press, thank you for enthusiastically and encouragingly embracing this manuscript. I am so grateful for your support and encouragement. You two are the reason it sings.

Table of Contents

Phoenix-Tongue

for my family,
the source of songs, my very blood

PHOENIX-TONGUE

...for dust thou art, and unto dust shalt thou return.
—Genesis 3:19

*As the days passed, my limbs turned purple and my face
turned to the colour of dust.*
—Kazuko Yamashima, atomic bomb survivor

Suppose we are not made of fire. Suppose we turn
children to dust. Should we carry their ash in an urn
as if the sacred exists? What some refer to as love
others burn as fuel. How should families speak of
paper and people enduring the feral infernos?
I ache with no choice. I shower with shadows
scarred on the walls. On my lover's stomach,
I lace a poem with my lips. Which will last: the width

of saliva, the sonnet, or her skin? Answer
the question in phoenix-tongue. The towers
collapsed on my birthday, and a crimson bird
built a nest in a tree. We were kids then, sure,
but how do you explain this—we set the nest ablaze.
One egg cooked in the center. The rest we saved.

I

INSECT, INFLICT

Too young to understand
the relationship between
scream and squirm, we thought

the bisected earthworm
felt no pain, believed crickets
could survive a split thorax

or crushed back legs.
What do we call that
form of innocence,

the childhood-specific
cruelties we inflict?
In the spring, my father

emerged from a bar fight,
a slash across his gut
like an open cocoon.

His shirt wet with blood,
mottled like a rotten leaf,
he survived. He smoked

while the ambulance
panicked down Main Street.
At home we watched

a dragonfly freed
of its wings,
its body

snipped
like the end of a plump
brown cigar.

INHERITED MUSIC

Because grey clouds gorge on themselves,
we intuitively know rain

will be the byproduct. Below them
starving palominos stomp the fallow field.

If you believe the stories
my mother bequeathed,

then you trust the shrinking skin
against their further protruding ribs

composes an eerie music, a lullaby
with ominous lyrics. It explains why

she so often crept to the barn and fell
asleep beside these creatures

while they stood lock-kneed and slumbering.
Somewhere in their stomachs, a song

you'd only sing at a child's funeral.
I never heard it, nor did I hear my mother

speak repeatedly about her mother
dying because I was deaf

with youth. At home, she nearly faded
into the beige sofa. A lit cigarette abandoned

itself to ash. There's my mother

leaning into the frayed corner of a throw pillow.

And I enter the room brashly, asking
about dinner, singing

a stupid song
I just heard on the radio.

ON THE BRANCH A BIRD WE BID GOODBYE

I boxed my father's vinyl
and stored them in the bloated sun

of Minnesota. I was an adolescent
who mistook light

for safety. It was the year
I ran away and learned warmth

deforms what we hold dear.
I returned three days later. Five a.m.

and the wrens chirped my arrival.
Most mornings no one wakes up

to welcome you with music,
but when I opened the door

my father flew off the recliner,
his expression warped from weeping.

On the phonograph my favorite tune
warbled like a sick bird

as I tried to mend
the wrinkles on his face

like stems
I carelessly snapped.

INSTRUMENTS ONLY HEARD AT NIGHT

What musician plays
fearlessly into the void?

Answer: not one
among the cluster of virtuosos

who learned the scales so well
they dreamt exclusively in song.

Dearest instruments,
when you were born

the world replaced sleep
with sonatas, and I didn't realize how

precious a note could be
until it was played

with the proper embouchure.
I now believe in harmony

the way Beethoven believed
the applause he could not hear

following the premier
of the Ninth Symphony.

No sound
undulated through

the kazoo of his cochlea.
He wept, betrayed by the ear.

Do children hear us
chanting their names like a charm

versus the deafness
we ultimately become? We sing

the minor key of existence,
and when our final chord fades

may the audience in the auditorium
clap wildly. May silence

like a gong
hiding in the balcony strike

anyone who dares to stop.

SOME NIGHTS THE STARS THEY SOUR

One hears a strand of hair
singed by flame—this, too, a song

that reminds us how swiftly music
turns to stench.

I spent weeks tuning
the smell. It was as useless as my mother

after her mother died—years pass and still
so heartbroken she plucks & burns

every grey curl she finds, moving only
to empty the ashtray.

~

Some nights the stars they sour
air with light.

We battle silence with a bottle
of wine, drink enough

to find darkness
profound. I tell you this

because it explains why sunrise
stalls on the horizon like a car

built before our birth—although we don't
recognize the make, we recognize the smoke

from the tailpipe
as something breaking down.

~

Call me a thief
when I lift my sick daughter from the bed

without the sheets noticing.
What time is it? None of us are dead yet

so I believe it's still early, and chirping
nourishes the morning. Little bird, little god of flight,

land on the branches
of my splintered fingers. Do you remember

our inheritance, our names? I whisper them
as a reminder; hear and know. Here and now,

slit your feathered throat
so you pronounce us properly.

ELEGY/TONGUE

When clouds suffocate the stars
we take comfort
in saying *alabaster*

out loud, flirt with the power
of our tongues.
Your lips flutter. The exhaled syllables

tickle me. This is how we combat
the empty baby seat
we refuse to remove from the car.

Our daughter is dead
tired. Say *luminance*. She will
not wake, not even when the word

brightens our mouths, twinkles
above her closed eyes.
Say *morning*. Say

good morning. No matter
how many times you declare it,
this appalling night lingers.

~

On other nights the moon
is a drop of spilt milk
pooled on an oil slick. It's enough

to illuminate a young girl

crawling out of a van.
In daydreams I abolish

the man beside her
who drags her back, whose fists root
like an infant's mouth.

I subtract the girl's dress
from the backseat, add it to the freckles
sprinkled across her shoulders.
She hides them like letters
on the page of a diary.
It devastates me

how the man misunderstood
the message, how he massaged
the wet paper to pieces.

The girl sputters in tongues,
and nobody is holy.
Someone told me

if you turn tragedy into story
you can survive it. I know
better. I'm no better.

~

Say *daybreak*. Say *break* again.
Nothing changes.

The night doesn't splinter
into spikes of brilliance.

~

Lick my cheek.
You'll taste dust and salt.

A tongue understands death
in ways neither of us is capable of.

Do you recall wagging yours
in the snowstorm, the fat flakes
blending into spit?
What you learned from that hybrid

cannot be stated, but nonetheless
remains true.

~

We could not see
what the forest witnessed.
The young girl inched toward the highway

and spoke in a voice
no one recognized.
It was Wednesday. My wife said

I was talking in my sleep.
I repeated *angel*
and *worm*, the words

the young girl wrote
when help arrived
too late.

My wife thought of
cake, silk.
I woke, trekked to the kitchen

to pour a glass of milk.
Angel.
Worm.

I crumbled and crawled
back to bed, back into the indent
of my body.

~

No one understood
the message. The police found the man

five miles from the scene. He kept
babbling, a brook

of nonsense flowing from his mouth
while the girl's tongue

lay on the shore of the passenger seat
like a slice of raw fish,

the rest of us
swept up in the torrent.

FUNERAL FOR SOMEONE I DON'T MISS

I

My shadow yawns along the wall
because the body tires

of light. Challenge me—prove this
is not the way

time fails us.
Isadora blots the silence

with babble the way bubbles
fill space. She wobbles.

Now her smaller shadow,
swallowed by mine,

wrecks me
with its disappearance.

II

I can't explain how birds
abandon gravity or why

their escape into sky
moors me into earth ever deeper.

In the woods we examine
the gnarled knuckle of a nest.

The branches clench
a mouse's skeleton. My daughter asks

where the rest of it sleeps:
the nose, the whiskers.

I wrestle with the answer
because she remembers every tenderness

taken from her. She eventually forgets
the question,

crushes leaves underfoot
like delicate bones.

III

When my daughter whimpers
in her sleep

I jolt awake. I am afraid
of the dreadful things she dreams:

a dog with an octopus beak, earthworms
where fingers should be.

When I enter the room she cries
even harder

while I hover overhead,
a helpless eclipse.

Last week a queue of mourners
shuffled toward a coffin,

a smear of black.
A child descended

into the dirt—the son
of a friend's friend.

That night I hooked
my fingers into my wife as if sex

disarms death, but death is not
the criminal; I am—the father

who attended a funeral
for a child he didn't miss.

PORTRAIT OF MY FATHER, SHIRTLESS

Before they shaved my father's chest,
before they pumped that disco ball

into a crowded dancehall
in his rhythm-dumb heart, I snapped

a picture of him shirtless, focused
on the white hairs curling from the lens

as if embarrassed. I watched the nurse
race a razor against his chest.

He did not bleed. We were not the same.

ELEGY/SOUND

Then there will be a loud cry throughout the whole land
of Egypt, such as has never been or will ever be again.
—Exodus 11:6

I

I lost the sound of traffic.

Screeching brakes like a hawk
hurt. Horns haunt

the suburbs. The fan
whirs, stirs dust in circles.

The day arrives on tiptoes
of light. I'd trade the sun
for one murmur of your mouth.

Say *horse*. Say *lion*. Chant *heavy*
three times
like you did when I carried you

from sedan to bedroom.

II

Think of Egypt, their great lament. . .

the ringing

in your ears

in the silence that follows

gives comfort.

III

Shower as if water
understands grief,
loss like a lather on your skin.

A pond makes a sound
unlike a lake, opposite

an ocean. Pay attention. The sea
froths at the mouth.

Waves no longer
      sound like an
            audience cheering.

IV

I lost the sound of—

Speak. Say *faculty*, say *pugnacious*.

Two vast hands of the Red Sea
clench, collapse.
A soldier remembers

                    laughter
from his clapping firstborn.
All this before

the slaughter, before
the ear plugs of rushing water.

We listen so severely to the sea
as it drones and drowns

everything out.

BECAUSE YOUR FATHER DIED ON OUR ANNIVERSARY

This morning I kissed your forehead,
and when your eyes opened I thought
what miracle, what terror.
On this day I don't make love
so much as make desperation

seem romantic. You wonder why I touch you
with intense reverence. It's because your father
and I are composed of shadow,
your body entirely of light.
I can only get so close before I, too,

disappear. Do you recall
the last time he chuckled or at what?
I remember how he slipped
into death like a man
plunging into a half-frozen lake.

Tonight, a blinking red light can break your heart.
The clouds drive across the horizon—
a funeral procession. You think of him
on our anniversary.
You see our play half-over, I see it

half-begun. We ask your father for directions
past the heavy curtains backstage.
No line, no matter how well written,
will be relevant enough to hold us here.
We're meant to leave this world with everyone

wanting so much more.

ON ONE HAND HILLSIDES AND HOUSES,

hornets hovering near hydrangeas.

Months of my youth squandered,
reaching for the other hand

until I shook with frustration,
unable to grasp it.

On a hillside, inside one house, passed out,
my father sprawled on the cat-torn couch, snoring.

His drinking is a kind of peace
the way a pacemaker is a kind of heart.

What an expert I am
at crawling on the carpet, cleaning up bottles

sheltered under his palm like a bumbershoot.
Bourbon Breath, Beer Belly. For the boy I was

both surnames for beauty
and blunder. Both bound me

until the other hand crept
past the gaping window, closed my father's eyes,

and ripped from the house my frame.
On this palm, bees bump me

as they stumble in flight, drunk
off nectar. I advise them

alight, sleep. The morning brings more pollen,
more sweetness, but serenity

we receive in doses
as if through the sting of syringes.

It only envelops the mind at rest
and while the hive remains

distant, our own buzzing is muffled.

BLIZZARD, 1996

I. What We Told Our Son
   (in the voice of the father)

Because the bitch was sick with age,
would not survive

another season. Because she stopped
eating the bits & scraps of meat

we gave her. Because the blizzard approached
like a buzzard to a corpse

and a good flurry makes the most beautiful
animal burial, merciful

as it throws itself down
handful after handful.

II. Through a Window Blurred by Moisture
    (in the voice of the mother)

The dense silence ensuing the gunshot
makes me question

whether I heard the noise at all.
Then, the shriek of my son

like a rabbit maimed, the creaking
front door, the stomping of my husband

clearing snow off his boots.
I watch a cloud curl

out of my howling son's mouth
and wonder about wounds

in the dead
of winter, whether steam rises from them

against the falling snow.

A NEST IN FOUR SEASONS
(Summer in the Voice of the Mother)

The manner in which a golden leaf
lands on sodden dirt—the mother's hand

hesitating
                    an instant before it strikes

her child's cheek. This, too, a mark
of tenderness.

A sharp slap, a yelp,
then a gasp from each of them.

The son runs outside while the mother
stares at her hand

as if it were a withered fruit
hung from her wrist.

       ~

The mother deciphers
the tracks of a fox

while the boy sucks
on icicles,

the woods now shushed by snow.
Beneath the trees, their breath

climbs the bark.
Steam tangles in the twigs

like the locks of Absalom,
the lovely, snarled son.

~

From the porch they watch
the sky, a feast of stars
on purple cloth.
The son forgets
the sting of the slap.
The mother forgets

to wash the filthy pots
stinking in the sink.
Instead she pulls him close,

kisses his cheek
while they listen to crickets chirp.
The moon hatches

a stillness around them,
and they breach it with laughter
like plants breaking soil.

~

Verbalize the wisdom
of acorns and of blessed things.

Estimate the sparrow's weight
upon the leaf-lush branch.

Observe the limb's shallow dip;
that is the worth of regret.

Here in the wilderness: epic space
and wind your escape plan.

You were once an egg, but don't mistake me
for a nest; I entered the world

a beak. I pecked at the shell
in order to push you out.

ELEGY/ECHO

I want to steal from a thousand movies

the scene where a woman
        screams and that
        scream delivers an infant,

an echo from a red cavern.

The scream, the baby,
both born from the body,

both sovereign now and fading
no matter how loud the cry.

~

In this scene, the infant wails and the mother won't wake

because all sound travels

from its source,

the direction

always

away.

~

Say the word. Say the word
and we'll rewind
the spool

of film.
No scream.   No echo.
         No body
leaving a body
torn, bloody.
Just a woman
smiling and speaking.

This footage proves my mother once spoke
the syllables of my name

in broken English. In broken English

my mother once spoke
and held my body close.
From her then a whimper, then farther
her voice traveled.

From her
            this world,
                        this mangled sentence.

ALTERATIONS

I

Bottom hemmed. Sleeves shortened.

Before leaving the shop
                 my mother waves

the tailor back, asks
for the remaining fabric
after the alterations.

I never bought a dress
this expensive.
I want to keep it all.

II

Turquoise with decorative pearls,

                picture tropical
                oceans & mussels

infected, the dress my mother wore
to my wedding, later

                     to her funeral.

III

I danced with my mother's head
bobbing
                by my chest.

My father drifts,   buoyant
with champagne, me his youngest
dancing in a white tuxedo—foam

overwhelmed by the water
of its creation.

ROAD TRIP, 1983

My father fills the water bottle
before the bugle call of dawn.

He is meticulous, each suitcase
labeled with our names and address.

Every summer our vacation
begins with a road trip

like a four-hour yawn
and my father flushed by noon

with vodka he disguises
as Evian. He spoils us

with gas station snacks:
Moon Pies, Twinkies, the whole family

jawing on jerky. On some
dusty road 90 miles from home

he asks if I want to take the wheel.
I am five and terrified

of tumbleweeds, road kill, the stillness
of an unanswered question.

My mother sleeps
in the backseat, my baby brother

just a bump in her belly.
He is home wherever she travels,

and I am in the old station wagon,
unsure whether to answer

yes or no, what direction
my father is headed, how fast

our house
disappears behind us.

DEEP WOUND SINGING

I

A brown buck shot in the side.
A son who days ago said

pulling a trigger frightened him the same way thunder
did as a toddler. And now childhood and blood

populate the spoor, mar the blades of grass
and stain the desolate woods

with their strange brand of harmony.

~

The father stalks the blotches, the bulk
of a dying beast

cacophonous, so much so the son
cries in his bed, prays

he never again shuffles—
as if chained— behind his father,

the world linked in a primal song
pulsing from the blood.

The anxious son
in the dark of his room

dreams himself to the center of a field
soaked in that darkness.

II

The boy shudders out of sleep, the girl
beside him pale & nude. He remembers

last night's moon. Still he thinks
of the buck, how it struggled downhill

toward the river as if called. He listens
for that song until the sun ignites

the girl's yawn. Her eyes open
like an eclipse passing.

He notices blood on his fingers,
on his thighs. The girl is humming

into his chest as if the heart heard
music. Her first time, she'd warned,

and although she'd bled,
she thanks him for it.

A SOUND WHICH CLEAVES

What lean muscle, what silk-breath
so easily moves the hairs of his arms.

What chapped lips like strips of ice
over a stream. What spring thaw, cracked

to reveal something wet. What blood.
What paranoia, what tidal pull

triggers the ebb and flow
beneath those closed lids. From his temple I want

to tongue the ghost-taste of salt.
What worship and troubled sleep.

What provocation of music
enters his dream, his pulse like a buck

racing with song until it is my flesh
he keeps pace with.

While I gazed at the moon
he came inside me

and something inside me
tore loose. What cadence we shared,

a simultaneous throb through our bodies,
panic and pleasure latticed within us.

Last evening everyone gathered
to watch the demolition

of a building, and each explosion arrived
nearly unwelcome in our chests, echoed

in the chamber of our bodies
until a moan pried open my mouth,

the dissonance of a doe
splitting herself to give birth—

which is to say I never heard
the raw wound of that sound

though who would ever doubt
such damage exists?

II

ELEGY/ELK RIVER

I

You will get lost so let me explain—

head down Main Street
where a rabid dog like a tyrant
was shot by the frightened townsfolk.

Take a left when you reach the dirt road.
There's a bright red house
and its porch light summons a moth.

Inside, a mother stirs garnet liquid
in a black pot. She tastes the fluid
sweet on her fingertips;

it's the same way small town boys
taste their first beer in a clearing.
They drink too much. They wobble

toward the sway of what they think
is a rope swing. When they arrive
one boy screams, the other stumbles

on upturned roots as he darts.
A third buckles, stunned
like a bird ignorant of glass.

II

It's late, and you're still here
so we may as well take the shortcut
across the cleat-wrecked field

behind my old high school.
Sneak beneath the third set of bleachers
where a girl named Alex

showed me once her naked chest
and beyond the seats to the forest
where she hung herself from an elm.

I knew her mother as a lover
of hummingbirds. When I heard
Alex covered herself

in homemade nectar, naturally
I thought of a feeder.
I brought her mother flowers

that withered overnight.
If you hear the moon's lament,
its loon-cry ululation

endemic to loss, then you've entered
Elk River. Take a peek.
Now turn around. Go back.

There's no more to see.
I can give you directions home,
but I've been here most of my life

and am no less lost. My neighbors
offer coffee and leftover cake.
It's a kindness, sure, but beware of the kind

of violence found only in lures:
the twirl of colored feathers,
the bob and weave of barb and hook.

Not every movement is dance,
not everything swallowed
sustenance.

ISAAC NEWTON'S TEETH

When I was young I flicked
my father's flimsy earlobes

as if they were fat little bells,
and I was happy.

Then one day I stopped.
Or he left. I don't know enough

about the order of things
to say which came first.

The smallest force
creates a chain of events

we shackle to the ankle of our futures.
You've heard this, too:

the monarch's wings, delicate
to the point of nonexistence,

breath by breath cause
a microburst across the world.

How much worse the damage then
caused by the whip tip

of a finger
stinging and stinging a father?

~

Our ignorance often
accelerates us.

So much of what we know
of motion

propelled by what we don't know
about impact. Newton

was born three months after
his father died.

Everything the scientist learns
amounts to a speck

of black pepper
reacting against his father's teeth,

those small canvases
of absence.

THE MEMORY OF GLASS

I

When I speak of the sacred
I conjure the exact scarlet

of a tanager

ruined by the windshield
of an oncoming car.

I contemplate the scar
immortalized in skin. I meditate

on the mother

throwing a glass that shatters
against her son's forearm

and never stops breaking.

II

When the word *mother*
tucks itself under my tongue, it is because I am scared
of invoking sacrifice, of releasing
those wings flinching toward fire.

And when I speak of fire,
I mean blood
rising out of wood, branches

that blanch the darkness.

When I was a child, I was haunted
by shadows. With a flashlight
my mother shaped them into animals
projected onto walls:
barking dog, timid rabbit, flying bird.

She then eclipsed the bulb
with her palm. Her skin glowed
ruddy with blood.

Only now do I understand light
illumines the sacred.

III

The memory of glass
is sand and searing lightning.
The memory of the scar
is blood released from the forearm
of the son, and the son

remembers himself
through infinite versions
down to the singular vision of a baby
not yet free of the womb.

And the mother. . . what does she remember?

Not a glass
hurled upon the son

but a crystalline bird
diving toward a vulnerable, sacred creature
she knew

it could never hold onto.

BOIL

I know things. For instance,

when I talk to certain men
about how a hummingbird's tongue

laps up nectar, their eyes
donut-glaze, and they bore a hole

clean through to the core
of me, right where I hide

my secret-self like the pit

of a cherry. I'm not psychic,
but I know what they're thinking.

I also know the exoskeleton
of a cricket

is cousin to the jaw harp,
but one plays music for the moon,

the other for the sun.
I listened to one chirp,

caught between the screen
and bedroom window.

For days I listened, feeling awful
for my curiosity, needing to know

what happens when we're trapped.
Some nights I hear hissing

from my mother's stove.
Her homemade nectar boils over

on the hot coils, bright red snakes
laying eggs of steam. I know heat;

I know how to hatch anything.

ONE CLOUD IN THE MOUTH OF THE SKY

I cried at the sight of a cow heart
seemingly beating on a metallic tray—

the sheer size of its chambers,
the boys too eager to finger them.

I didn't touch it
though I wanted to.

When the teacher left the room
a pack of students

forced me in the closet
and placed the grey organ

at my feet. While the kids
laughed and laughed

I sat down and listened
to an awful thumping in my ears,

confused
about whose heart it was.

When the teacher returned,
the closet slid open

and beyond the window
I spotted

the bright throb of blue sky
with one cloud

marring it, a dead dove
in the mouth of a stray.

BLESSING OF SCABS

None of us were mean enough
to rip up the dead leaves
in front of the old woman

who gave them away like gifts,
but none too kind to keep them
either. And I was

too embarrassed to say
how pretty they were,
symmetrical and red

like autumn's answer
to the lobster.
She treated each leaf

as a precious thing
and our parents told us she wasn't
right in the head. My buddy

crushed them in his palms,
sprinkled the brittle flecks
onto our scalps like a blessing

of scabs. Lately I've been thinking
about the holy,
why saints aren't named saints

until they're dead. It makes a dumb sense
the same way I tell my dad
I love him by punching him, how he leaves

an occasional beer in the garage
and doesn't question its ghost
haunting my breath. The first time

my friends and I got drunk
was in the dim of the forest
behind the high school. Lit

by the moon, a rope swing
in the distance, swaying. We ran,
bark blurring on our periphery,

and we saw everything in twin:
two swings, two trees.
And like those leaves both beautiful

and worthless, like blood thickened
to scab, the world appeared
balanced by its doppelgänger.

Then one friend stumbled,
gnarled roots like a bully's foot,
the other screamed out

Jesus, Jesus, and me not noticing
a woman hanging from a tree limb,
shouting eagerly toward death

Me first, me first.

RESIDUE

If the couple were to touch the dead cat
they would find it warm, blood cooling
in twilight's glow. If the pavement were
an area rug, it would appear serene

and the couple walking wouldn't stop
to stare, wouldn't tremble slightly.
Poor darling. We have to move it.
The man scowls, threatens to leave,

though doesn't step any further.
Please, the woman pleads, *what if. . .*
(Years later, a girl recalls her pet, wondering
if the mangled thing was really him.) *For her sake.*

The man cracks a branch off a tree,
pushes the animal carefully to the side of the road.
For a moment he is afraid the cat might burst,
convinced he saw something shift inside

as if death were a verb, somehow alive
and hiding in the bowels. The feline lies crumpled
closer to the sidewalk, fur an oily black,
a sponge absorbing the abundant night.

She touches the man's shoulder
as a thank you. He glares straight ahead
until he gets her home. He refuses the invitation
for tea, exchanges quick goodbyes and a kiss.

The woman watches through the open door,
hoping he'll turn back and spend the night,
praying he'll be safe when he doesn't.
He disappears down the empty street.

Alone at home he pours a drink. He remembers
the weight of the animal—a bag of sugar,
the twig pressing into his palm, the sap
still sticky even after he washes.

A SUBTLE COLLAPSE

I peck like a crow
the scattered crumbs of silence
until I'm outside, hungry for quiet
by a tree whose branch
stretches to obscure
a lamppost, the lamp
illuminating the trunk.

~

The sprinklers spray ceaselessly
despite the rain. The ground
gives in—a subtle collapse.

I'm not familiar with mud.

Where I grew up, the earth remained
frozen or dry.

There were no times between.

~

There's a clunk, then the clink
of ice cubes skittering out of a glass.
Something on the rocks
dribbles over the counter.

Last night was strange, Lydia says,
I hated it.

I wear the phone booth like a trench coat
against the promise I broke.

I ask her to pay attention
to the exact moment
ice becomes liquid.

~

What I can tell you is this:
the red-headed boy running circles
around a dry, fallen leaf
tires eventually. His overweight mother

sits on the stone bench, rubs his back
over the orange shirt
when he crumples next to her
sweating, the world
out of breath.

TSUNAMI

Since she died gradually, I thought her death
like spilt honey

would be easy to manage, the viscous mess
slow, controllable.

Over the course of months
the senses one at a time went

blind, the words next,
each flung from her mouth

then shot
as if by skeet shooters

until conversation was impossible, until only
the lone word *water*

croaked from her throat.
Then organs like shops in a bankrupt mall

pulled down their shutters,
taped up handwritten thanks.

Now the flat line sings with the steady force
of a tsunami. It intones a note, escalates

in amplitude.
It overwhelms—not with precision but totality—

streetlamps and identical offices,
trees with their frail leaves

frantically paddling against the waves.
All bodies transform

to water and rubble
when confronted with water and rubble.

Listen: In the beginning
was the mother, and the mother

covered her child.
In the end was the child who covered the mother.

In all the sacred stories, there is this blanket we clutch—
the color of milk, the color of foam.

KITE

The stripper grinds her ass
into the man's groin

like she's smothering a fire,
moans *You're so hot, so*

exotic, asks *What race are you?*
and he replies Seattle Marathon

for a cheap chuckle then states,
breathless, half-Japanese, *Oh,*

I love Asian men! and *Would you
like another dance?* and *On your*

mother's side? and the man says
yes and yes, but

she died recently, and the stripper
straddles him, coos *Sweetie, I'm sorry*

and hugs him, her enormous breasts
embracing his face

which hardens to a cliff
then erodes, chunks

crumbling into the lunatic sea,
and on that cliff a boy

dangerously close to tumbling over
and behind him his mother

jerks him back the way we pull
the string of a kite

and it rises, it rises, look
dear and distant woman,

at the things we cherish,
how quickly they fly out of reach.

THE SPIDER WEAVER

If you believe her story then you believe sunlight
is enough to save us,

that we, too, can climb legs of light
up to the immense embrace of heaven.

Kids in Japan know a young farmer
drove off a hungry snake

from devouring a spider. And later,
the sun stretched down the ladder of his leg

and rescued the same spider from the same
hungry snake. The grateful arachnid

wove cloth for the farmer, clouds
for the empty sky. *Kumo* means "spider"

or "cloud." Repeat it and it switches
smoothly without us knowing

the way God's face turned
to a nuclear blast for those who believed

the light they saw would save them.

LIFE SENTENCE

My friend phoned in the morning—
two months pregnant
and already her baby was dead.

Weak heart, she sobbed.
Stack every dictionary from every library
and still nothing balances

such a phrase. Two words
scar the face of the world
like a botched surgery.

Think of those phrases so dense
we hunch from the weight of them:
missing person, suicide pact, human

trafficking. Yet I offered
this pairing: take care—hardly enough
to hoist a single anchor of pain

docking her marooned frame.
Language shatters under scrutiny
the way a sesamoid might

on a galloping horse.
But we continue to scramble
like Ruffian after she woke

from the operation, opening wounds,
and creating new ones. We race
for a *life sentence*, something

with sufficient voltage
to shock soul back into muscle,
a phrase driven like a chariot

to trample the awful lexicon of loss.
Meanwhile, when *I* and *do*
strike together, we ignite—

tenderness turning us to tinder.
Everyone begs for that fire,
but years ago we watched

as squirrels and deer
darted into a forest clearing.
It wasn't the animals that stunned us—

it was the insatiable heat beyond,
how we knew instinctively
nobody could survive

that kind of joy.

Note: Ruffian was a champion thoroughbred racehorse
who was euthanized due to injuries.

RITUALS OF COMFORT

I. Monday

Tomorrow determines my belief
in mercy   or misery.
Meanwhile, I gamble
the trust Jordan places in me.
I throw a pair of dice

at cancer. I bet a single cube of flesh
sliced from her lover's arm.

My wife busies herself
with boiling water for tea,
fetching blankets and pillows,
the ordinary
                rituals of comfort.

We coil around two conversations:
one a rattlesnake, the other a licorice wheel.
Hours later and Jordan ambles
into sleep, trailing tissues
on our worn couch.

I'm convinced the wind
prophesies the future, so I leave
the window ajar,
let it creep between the screen and me,
watch it move Jordan's hair
without rousing her—a secret tenderness.

II. Tuesday

With the sun barely peeking
into our home, I overhear
my wife quietly singing
in the living room.
She strokes Jordan's hair,
tucks it behind her ears.

My wife obliges our friend in a hymn.
They close their eyes.

I close mine, too, and think
of an article
                        concerning group suicides,

how three students
burned

charcoal briquettes in an empty apartment.

All three wore
ski goggles
to keep the smoke from their eyes.

WHAT NEVER BREAKS

I

In the hospital, my father worked hard
to deliver
himself over to death, his face
a dingy pearl on the pillow.

His chest rattled like a toy
filled with little forks. His fever
spiked. With each breath

our family like anchors
reeled closer to the body,
and with each breath he pushed
the soul further out like a boat
we wanted desperately to keep ashore.

II

God, like an architect,
built us from wishbones,
so if you ever break one,
whatever you want is yours.

A fairytale my father wove
like a faulty safety net.

Because I was adventurous
and clumsy as a kid, I climbed
a gnarled tree in our backyard

then fell as dull as an acorn
onto the grass. Several seeds
splintered inside my fingers and wrist.

I wished the pain would stop
growing like a cactus up my arm
and immediately

I knew my father was a liar.

III

With the moon exposed amid the clouds
like a compound fracture, I wander
the flat fields of his backyard.
A spring mist fingers my flesh
as if playing a piano
on fire. I toast the furcula,

break down in the mud, and splatter
in the puddles like a bird bathing.
By the time I return
I look like a rook.

I cower under covers,
an egg beneath a mother bird, hiding
from everything I fear
will never break.

FOREST OF NO TREASURE

I slit my wrist before leaving
my childhood

so I can hike my way back. Never will I age

again. I hijack the nomadic pirate ship
of this scarred body

and float
                    in the forest of no treasure.

If I steer toward a path
splotchy with blood, will I discover

my mother's crooked smile,
see her breathe gently over the toes

of the newborn I once was?

Someone buried the answers
in the crocodile's belly,

but I sail from his gnashing teeth. I don't stop
until my alarm slaps me senseless
like the shimmering tail of a mermaid.

Enter the evening of low sunsets,
where mothers croon

lullabies from Neverland,
the ones sung

to smother the rustling

of children crying. Mrs. Darling
opens a window and spreads a blanket,
but her tender face has no vacancy
for a kiss—my lips parted, orphaned.

MESROBIANS GO THRIFTING

for Carrie Mesrobian

In other words we sift through the sad lives
of the tasteless, their grotesque

paintings of bald eagles and motorcycles.
In other words box after box of dust

and flannel shirts. A frame chipped by a tooth
and that tooth, too, marked down. In other words

a sale on the very things that define us.
Someone in the book aisle

thumbs through a used Limbaugh
and cannot stop himself

from quoting and laughing, quoting and laughing.
In other words dull tools.

In other words pink pencil sharpeners, erasers
grinding away every mistake

we pawn onto others. In other words
a candle that glows the halo

of Mother Mary, and her Son, and whatever
Father. In other words what father.

In other words no words
exchanged in some time

and there is a rotary phone
I pick up and dial

zero zero zero zero
and watch all those boulders

roll back to the bottom of that hill
where my father is buried and I ask how

are you to the air and are
you happy and of course no

one answers and a clerk asks *everything
okay?* and I say it's only

a dollar and I'd take it if I knew
how to call home.

LIGHTHOUSE

Let me guide you home
with a lit cigarette as our lighthouse.
Steer clear of shoals, shallows
where rocks rip holes into skin-

thin hulls and ships
guzzle mouthfuls of water.
Waves cover rubble in foam
like steamed milk. I want to demonstrate

the loneliness of heating bottles
for my daughter.
I hum your name
as a cradlesong. Soon, she sinks

like a cannon ball into dreams.
Do you realize nothing we offer
anchors those we love
to us? The night you left

proves this. We simply keep watch
of their terrible rowing
and note the elegant cuts
their exodus marks on the surface.

I can fathom this much—
the scar slips
below the water, but the water
remembers. It weeps

alongside the shore and bare feet
of children who shout and point
to a lighthouse
retired so long ago

it barely recalls separating
light from dark, sea from harbor,
the ones who left from those on land
who wait anxiously through the star-soaked night

into the somber shipwreck of dawn.

Michael Schmeltzer was born and raised in Yokosuka, Japan before moving to the US. He is the author of *Elegy/Elk River,* winner of the Floating Bridge Press Chapbook Award. He earned an MFA from the Rainier Writing Workshop at Pacific Lutheran University. His honors include numerous Best of the Net and Pushcart Prize nominations, the Gulf Stream Award for Poetry, and the Blue Earth Review's Flash Fiction Prize. His writing has been published in various journals such as *Rattle, PANK, Mid-American Review,* and *Natural Bridge*, among others. *Blood Song* is his first full-length collection.

Publications by Two Sylvias Press:

The Daily Poet: Day-By-Day Prompts
For Your Writing Practice
by Kelli Russell Agodon and Martha Silano (Print and eBook)

The Daily Poet Companion Journal (Print)

Fire On Her Tongue:
An Anthology of Contemporary Women's Poetry
edited by Kelli Russell Agodon and Annette Spaulding-Convy
(Print and eBook)

The Poet Tarot and Guidebook:
A Deck Of Creative Exploration (Print)

Blood Song
by Michael Schmeltzer (Print and eBook)

Naming The No-Name Woman,
Winner of the 2015 Two Sylvias Press Chapbook Prize
by Jasmine An (Print and eBook)

Community Chest
by Natalie Serber (Print)

Phantom Son
by Sharon Estill Taylor (Print and eBook)

What The Truth Tastes Like
by Martha Silano (Print and eBook)

landscape/heartbreak
by Michelle Peñaloza (Print and eBook)

Earth, Winner of the 2014 Two Sylvias Press Chapbook Prize
by Cecilia Woloch (Print and eBook)

The Cardiologist's Daughter
by Natasha Kochicheril Moni (Print and eBook)

She Returns to the Floating World
by Jeannine Hall Gailey (Print and eBook)

Hourglass Museum
by Kelli Russell Agodon (eBook)

Cloud Pharmacy
by Susan Rich (eBook)

Dear Alzheimer's: A Caregiver's Diary & Poems
by Esther Altshul Helfgott (eBook)

Listening to Mozart: Poems of Alzheimer's
by Esther Altshul Helfgott (eBook)

*Crab Creek Review 30th Anniversary Issue
featuring Northwest Poets*
edited by Kelli Russell Agodon and Annette Spaulding-Convy
(eBook)

Please visit Two Sylvias Press (www.twosylviaspress.com) for information on purchasing our print books, eBooks, writing tools, and for submission guidelines for our annual chapbook prize. Two Sylvias Press also offers editing services and manuscript consultations.

Created with the belief
that great writing is good for the world.

Visit us online: www.twosylviaspress.com

CPSIA information can be obtained
at www.ICGtesting.com
Printed in the USA
FSHW011252060320
67880FS